SUMMARY:
ATOMIC HABITS

A BOOK BY JAMES CLEAR

30 MINUTE BOOK SUMMARIES

Other Books by
30 Minute Book Summaries

Summary: Start with Why

Summary: Leaders Eat Last

Summary: The Infinite Game

Summary: Leadership Classics 3-in-1 Collection

Summary: The 7 Habits of Highly Effective People

Summary: How to Win Friends & Influence People

Summary: Self Help Classics 2-in-1 Collection

Summary: The Miracle Morning

Summary: High Performance Habits

Summary: Success Habits 2-in-1 Collection

Summary: The Power of Habit

Contents

The Fundamentals:
Why Tiny Changes Make a Big Difference

The Surprising Power of Atomic Habits

Small improvements lead to big changes over time. By getting 1% better every day, you would be 37 times better at the end of one year. Unfortunately, these tiny improvements are hard to see in the short-term. It's easy to become discouraged and slip back into old habits.

What is most important is the trajectory of the path you are on. Your current results are less important than your current habits. Your results will always trail behind your actions. But if your habits are moving in the right direction, your results will follow in the same direction.

The path toward successful habit change has several bumps. During the early stages, it's hard to see any progress, and it's easy to become disappointed by the lack of results. With continued focus on the habit, a tipping point is reached—and the results seem to be an overnight success. It is important to remember, however, that the success was due to consistent effort over a period of time.

While most people recommend setting and pursuing specific goals, a better approach is to focus on the systems that lead to success. Goals have their place, establishing a vision of the future. Systems are even more important, as they provide specific steps toward achieving the goal.

How Your Habits Shape Your Identity (and Vice Versa)

Behavior change involves three layers:

1. Outcomes
2. Processes
3. Identity

Most people focus on changing the outcome. They set a goal for achieving a certain result. Some people try to change systems and processes. They alter what they do so that they can change their behavior. Very few people focus on changing their identity. These rare individuals emphasize the person they want to become in the future.

Habit change is most likely to last when those habits become part of a person's identity. Someone is more likely to stick with the habit of running if her goal is to become a runner — rather than having the goal of finishing a race. The second goal is a temporary achievement. The first goal provides a new identity that serves as a deeper motivation for continuing the habit of running.

Many people travel through their lives with negative identities. They have been told that they are not good enough in some way—maybe they're not a "morning person" or maybe they are habitually late. These negative identities make it much more difficult to maintain positive changes. They have a script constantly replaying in their heads, keeping them stuck in an old identity and in bad habits. The key, then, is to flip the script.

Changing your identity requires two steps:

1. Determine who you want to become
2. Confirm it with small wins

First, you must determine the person you want to become. Decide what purpose, values, and beliefs are central to that identity. For example, if you want to lose weight, you might choose to become a healthy person who eats nutritious food and exercises regularly.

Second, you must make decisions that are in alignment with that future identity. Using the previous example, when you are faced with a decision to eat junk food or to eat a healthy meal, ask yourself what a healthy person would eat. Choose to live consistently with your future identity. Achieving a new identity can only be accomplished through small, consistent victories over time.

How to Build Better Habits in 4 Simple Steps

Habits are automatic solutions to consistent problems. When the brain is faced with a particular situation multiple times, it creates habits to solve the problem with the least amount of energy possible. These habits are controlled at a subconscious level so that the conscious mind is free to address more pressing matters.

Habits involve four steps:

1. Cue
2. Craving
3. Response
4. Reward

A cue is a mental or physical trigger that sets the habit process into motion. The cue leads to a craving, a desire to achieve a certain internal state. The craving drives a response, which is the mental or physical routine that is central to the habit. The response leads to a reward, which is the immediate prize for completing the habit.

In order to form a good habit, you must make the habit:

1. Obvious
2. Attractive
3. Easy
4. Satisfying

Each of these four characteristics corresponds with one part of the habit process. Forming good habits requires an obvious cue. An attractive habit stimulates a craving. Good habits can only be formed when the response is easy. Finally, a satisfying reward ensures that the habit will be performed in the future.

To change a bad habit, you must make the habit:

1. Invisible
2. Unattractive
3. Difficult
4. Unsatisfying

Changing a bad habit is the exact opposite of forming a good habit. The cue is made invisible so that the habit is not initiated. When the habit is made unattractive, cravings are diminished. Making the habit difficult places a barrier in the way of the response. Finally, unsatisfying rewards decrease the likelihood of repeating the behavior in the future.

The 1st Law – Make It Obvious

The Man Who Didn't Look Right

Behavior change starts with awareness. Most habits occur subconsciously, so these routines must be identified so that habit change can occur.

The author recommends creating a Habits Scorecard, which involves two steps:

1. List your daily habits.
2. Identify each habit as positive (+), negative (-), or neutral (=) by marking it with the corresponding symbol.

The purpose of the Habits Scorecard is to create awareness, not to initiate changes. Review your habits without self-criticism or self-praise. This creates a foundation for the next step.

The Best Way to Start a New Habit

Research has shown that people are more likely to start a new habit, such as exercising, when they set a specific time and place to perform the routine. One study divided nearly 250 participants into three groups. The first group simply recorded each time they exercised. The second group was educated on the benefits of exercise in addition to recording their workouts. The third group was asked to establish a plan for exercising by filling in this statement, "During the next week, I will partake in at least 20 minutes of vigorous exercise on [Day] at [Time] in [Place]." Fewer than 40% of people in the first and second groups exercised as least one day per week. In contrast, more than 90% of the third group exercised at least one day per week.

The third group took advantage of a concept called implementation intention. This concept describes a process in which a person decides exactly how he will respond when a specific cue arises. By consciously creating a plan for responding to a specific cue, the person is more aware of the cue and is more likely to initiate his desired response—rather than the automatic response of the old habit.

Time and location are the most common cues that set our habits into motion. The author recommends the following statement for setting implementation intention: "I will [Behavior] at [Time] in [Location]." For example, you might state, "I will run for 30 minutes at 6 a.m. on my home treadmill." This goal has a specific behavior, time, and location. This specific plan greatly increases the likelihood of following through with the new habit.

Another way to incorporate a new habit is habit stacking. Habit stacking involves performing a new habit immediately after a current habit. In this way, the current habit serves as a cue to initiate the new habit. The author recommends the following statement for habit stacking: "After [Current Habit], I will [New Habit]." For example, you might state, "After brushing my teeth in the morning, I will run for 30 minutes on the treadmill."

Use the Habits Scorecard from the previous chapter to identify the best habits to stack with your new habit. Make sure that the cue is very specific and obvious. "After brushing my teeth" is a better cue than "in the morning" because it provides a specific stimulus that can trigger a specific response.

Motivation Is Overrated; Environment Often Matters More

Environment is one of the strongest influences on behavior. Psychologist Kurt Lewin stated, "Behavior is a function of the person in their environment." While most people believe that their bad habits are moral failures, those habits are largely influenced by the surrounding environment.

Dr. Anne Thorndike decided to test the impact of food location on food choices that were made in the cafeteria at Massachusetts General Hospital. She ensured that bottled water was placed in locations around the cafeteria, including the refrigerators by the cash registers. Over a three-month period, bottled water sales increased by 25.8%, while soft drink purchases fell by 11.4%. The actual product offerings were not changed. Only their locations were altered.

People respond to the obvious cues within their environment, with visual cues exerting a disproportionately large amount of influence on habits. One key to forming good habits is to prominently display the cue within your environment. If you want to start your day with a morning jog, place your running shoes by your bed so that you can immediately put them on. Another key is to provide multiple cues that will trigger your new behavior. In addition to putting your running shoes in a prominent location, you might place your workout clothes nearby as well. Another good use of environmental cues is to designate certain rooms—or spaces within rooms—for particular tasks. In the running habit example, you might have a specific exercise room that houses a treadmill.

New habits are easier to form in new environments. If you choose unhealthy products at your regular grocery store, go to another one. If spending most of your nights in the living room triggers a habit of binge-watching television, switch your routine so that you spend time in another room or outside. Subtle environmental changes can lead to substantial behavioral changes.

The Secret to Self-Control

Changing a bad habit requires making the cue invisible. Remove the cue that triggers the bad habit, and you are well on your way to kicking the habit.

Research in the 1970s revealed that 15-20% of American soldiers in Vietnam were addicted to heroin. Their environment was incredibly stressful, heroin was readily accessible, and their friends were taking up the habit as well. When those soldiers returned home, about 1 in 10 of these heroin addicts remained addicted to heroin. Researchers concluded that environment was the primary cue that contributed to the heroin addiction.

People who seem to have high levels of self-control don't have endless resources of willpower. Instead, they structure their environment in a way that requires very little willpower. Self-control can provide short-term wins, but environmental control ensures long-term success.

For each bad habit you want to eliminate, identify the cue and remove that cue from the environment. If watching television in your bedroom is interfering with your sleep, remove the television from the bedroom. If snacking on candy is causing you to gain weight, throw away the candy dish. Don't rely on self-control when changing your environment can eliminate the negative cue.

The 2ⁿᵈ Law – Make It Attractive

How to Make a Habit Irresistible

Making a habit seem attractive helps to stimulate the cravings that drive habits. The modern food industry has taken advantage of this concept to sell their products. They create irresistible flavors that balance salt, fat, and sugar. They utilize contrasting textures that create a mouthfeel that consumers love. Every aspect of their products is designed to stimulate a craving to consume even more of that product.

Cravings are related to the release of dopamine within the brain. In particular, dopamine is released in anticipation of receiving a reward, and the dopamine stimulates the brain to complete the habit.

Temptation bundling is one method for making habits more attractive. It involves performing an action that you need to do alongside an action that you want to do. Temptation bundling can also be combined with habit stacking.

The author recommends the following statement for the combination of temptation bundling and habit stacking: "After [Current Habit], I will [Habit I Need]. After [Habit I Need], I will [Habit I Want]." By connecting your new habit with something you already enjoy, you make the new habit more attractive.

The Role of Family and Friends in Shaping Your Habits

Many habits are established by the influence of cultural norms. In particular, people mimic those around them based on three factors:

1. Proximity
2. Number
3. Power

The closer someone is to you, the more likely that person is to influence your habits. People are more likely to become obese if they have obese friends. Children who have friends with high IQs show improvements in their own IQs three years later.

Take advantage of the influence of proximity on building good habits. Join a group where the good habit is the norm. Find a group where you share common interests with the group members. Group dynamics help you to establish a new identity that encourages new habits to take hold.

Larger groups of people exert greater influence than a smaller number of people. It is natural to look to others to determine what is normal behavior within a particular culture. Peer pressure influences behavior because people want to fit in with the group. Groups are an effective way to implement this concept as well.

Powerful people wield a tremendous amount of influence over the behavior of others. Most people imitate those in power because it increases their status within the culture. Seek to mimic the behaviors of people who possess the habits that you wish to have.

How to Find and Fix the Causes of Your Bad Habits

Changing a bad habit requires making it seem unattractive. This will minimize the craving, and the habit will be less likely to persist.

Cravings are solutions to deeper desires. When people mindlessly browse social media, their craving is linked to a deeper desire for connecting with others. Others smoke cigarettes due to a deeper desire to relieve stress. People don't crave social media or cigarettes; they crave connection and stress relief.

Bad habits can be changed by finding an alternative solution to the deeper desire. Smokers can go for a short walk to relieve their stress. Instead of browsing social media during a break at work, a person can interact in-person with coworkers to satisfy the need for connection.

Bad habits can also be altered by reframing the feelings associated with them. Recall the negative feelings that are produced by the bad habit and the positive feelings that result from avoiding that habit. Emphasize the benefits of avoiding the bad habit and the drawbacks of following the habit.

4

The 3rd Law – Make It Easy

Walk Slowly, but Never Backward

Many people confuse being in motion with taking action. Being in motion refers to planning stages, whereas taking action refers to implementation stages. Reading diet books is being in motion. Following a healthy diet is taking action. Finding the best exercise program is being in motion. Completing a workout is taking action.

People who are in constant motion—rather than taking action—are seeking a sense of progress without risking failure. It requires courage to take action, but being in motion is safe. In avoiding failure, they also avoid success.

The first step in making a habit easy is to simply perform the task over and over. Each repetition of a habit—whether a good habit or a bad habit—strengthens the brain connections associated with that habit. By performing a good habit as often as possible, you ensure that the habit becomes automatic in a short period of time.

The Law of Least Effort

The Law of Least Effort states that people will choose the easier option rather than the harder option. This allows them to conserve energy for other activities. By making it easy to perform good habits, you greatly increase the chances of that habit becoming automatic.

Optimizing the environment is perhaps the most effective method for making a good habit easy to perform. Set up the physical environment at home and work to minimize any obstacles to engaging in the habit. For example, improve your environment for your exercise habit by creating a separate workout space in your home. Add new habits to your regular daily routines, such as choosing a gym that is on the route between home and work.

The environment can also be set up in a way that discourages a bad habit. Increase the number of obstacles to performing the habit. If television watching is interfering with more important activities, you can unplug it after watching, remove the batteries from the remote, move the television to a closet, or all of the above. Find creative ways to design your environment so that bad habits are harder to perform.

How to Stop Procrastinating by Using the Two-Minute Rule

People face multiple decisive moments each day. These moments offer a choice—engage in a good habit or fall back into a bad habit. One good choice often leads to another good choice, and another. Likewise, one bad choice can lead to numerous other bad choices. In this way, small habit changes can lead to amazingly positive results.

When implementing a new habit, scale down the habit to fit into two minutes or less. Instead of meditating for 10 minutes, start with one minute. Instead of exercising for an hour, start with a two-minute routine. Completing these short tasks creates a sense of accomplishment and builds momentum for the future.

This "two-minute rule" prioritizes showing up. It emphasizes consistency over perfection. It builds the identity, not just the habit.

As the habit takes hold, you can add time to the length of the routine. The first two minutes serve as a warm-up for the longer practice. When extending the length of any routine, make sure to keep the time short enough that the task doesn't feel like work.

How to Make Good Habits Inevitable and Bad Habits Impossible

Changing a bad habit requires making it difficult. One method of increasing the difficulty of a bad habit is the use of a commitment device. A commitment device is a present decision about a future behavior. If your television watching habit prevents you from getting enough sleep, consider an outlet timer that automatically shuts off power to your television at a pre-programmed time each night. If you often avoid going to the gym, pre-pay for your membership so that each missed workout costs you money.

Technology can be a very effective tool in automating good habits and preventing bad habits. Automatic withdrawals from your paycheck can ensure that you're saving enough money. Turning off social media notifications can prevent distractions. Find creative ways to leverage technology to improve your habits.

5

The 4th Law – Make It Satisfying

The Cardinal Rule of Behavior Change

Good habits are built by making the habits satisfying. This satisfaction can be subtle, such as the case of handwashing in Pakistan. In the 1990s, the residents of Pakistan were suffering from widespread diseases. They knew that washing their hands was important, but few people washed their hands on a consistent basis. Stephen Luby, in partnership with Procter & Gamble, attempted to rectify this problem by providing residents with a foaming soap. Since this soap created a more satisfying experience, handwashing became commonplace. Public health was dramatically impacted, as diarrhea and pneumonia cases were cut in half.

Immediate satisfaction—not delayed satisfaction—is one of the keys to habit change. Unfortunately, good habits tend to be less satisfying in the present and more satisfying in the future. Bad habits, on the other hand, are often more satisfying in the present and less satisfying in the future. The goal of habit change is to increase the immediate rewards for good habits and to provide immediate pain for bad habits.

Rewards should reinforce the identity you are building. Your reward for completing an exercise routine might be a massage, not ice cream. Your reward for saving money might be a bubble bath, not a shopping spree. Immediate rewards that are tied to your identity will help build intrinsic motivation to continue the good habit.

How to Stick with Good Habits Every Day

Visual measures of progress can make habits more satisfying. Habit tracking is a particularly powerful method. Habit tracking involves recording a habit on a calendar and checking it off when the habit is completed for the day. This provides a visual cue to perform the habit and a satisfying reward when the task is completed.

Habit tracking should be:

1. Automated when possible
2. Limited to a few essential habits
3. Recorded immediately after the habit is completed

Since life gets in the way of habits on some days, it is essential to have a plan for preventing a relapse into bad habits. The easiest plan is to commit to never failing to perform the habit two days in a row. Even if the habit cannot be completed in full on the second day, it is important to show up and perform at least some of the task.

How an Accountability Partner Can Change Everything

Changing a bad habit requires making it unsatisfying. A habit contract sets out the immediate punishment for engaging in a bad habit. It is a written contract that lists the specific punishments for failing to stick to a habit, and at least one other person signs the contract to serve as an accountability partner. Having an accountability partner increases the stakes, as failing to complete a task leads to letting down someone else.

Advanced Tactics: How to Go from Being Merely Good to Being Truly Great

The Truth About Talent (When Genes Matter and When They Don't)

People are genetically predisposed to succeed in certain areas but not in other areas. These areas are usually the most satisfying for people, so it is important to find the tasks that you enjoy the most.

When trying a new activity, you will move through two phases—exploration and exploitation. In the exploration phase, you experiment with multiple ideas and activities until you find what works best for you. In the exploitation phase, you narrow your focus to that area where you are succeeded. Once you are successful in a certain area, you should devote 80-90% of your time to exploiting and 10-20% of your time to exploring.

The Goldilocks Rule: How to Stay Motivated in Life and Work

People maintain peak levels of motivation when the difficulty of a task is at the edge of their ability. If the task is too easy, they will get bored. If the task is too difficult, they will get frustrated and possibly give up. Challenge is essential to growth, but it must be a manageable challenge.

When an assignment challenges a person's ability just the right amount, the person can achieve what is called a flow state. She is fully immersed in the task. This flow state is achieved by selecting activities that are 4% beyond a person's current ability.

The Downside of Creating Good Habits

Good habits must be combined with deliberate practice to achieve mastery in a certain area. Good habits provide subconscious control of easy tasks. Deliberate practice trains for achievement of more difficult tasks that require conscious thought.

Since habits are subconscious by nature, it is easy to fall into a trap of stagnation and contentment. The antidote to this is consistent reflection on your habits. The author recommends two periods of reflection each year—an annual review in December and an "integrity report" in June. The annual review looks at the things that went well, the things that didn't go well, and the things that you learned over the previous year. The integrity report assesses whether your actions are in alignment with your identity.

The 30 Minute Workbook

The 18 questions on the following pages will help you apply the lessons from Atomic Habits.

Take a few minutes to reflect on each question. Write down your answers in the space provided or on a notebook of your own.

The Fundamentals

1. Habit change is most likely to last when those habits become part of your identity. What identity do you want to adopt? List three values or beliefs that are central to that identity

_____

_____

_____

_____

_____

_____

_____

_____

_____

The Fundamentals

2. Are you living in alignment with that identity? Which actions are in alignment? Which actions are out of alignment?

_____

_____

_____

_____

_____

_____

_____

_____

_____

_____

The 1ˢᵗ Law – Make It Obvious

3. Create a Habits Scorecard by listing your daily habits and marking each habit with (+), (-), or (=).

The 1st Law – Make It Obvious

4. List three good habits you want to develop using the implementation intention method. Use the sentence structure: "I will [Behavior] at [Time] in [Location]."

_____

_____

_____

_____

_____

_____

_____

_____

_____

_____

The 1ˢᵗ Law – Make It Obvious

5. List the previous three good habits using the habit stacking method. Use the sentence structure: "After [Current Habit], I will [New Habit]."

_____

_____

_____

_____

_____

_____

_____

_____

_____

_____

The 1st Law – Make It Obvious

6. For your three good habits, how can you establish obvious cues in your environment to trigger the habit?

_____

_____

_____

_____

_____

_____

_____

_____

_____

The 1st Law – Make It Obvious

7. List one bad habit you want to remove. How can you eliminate the cue for that habit?

_____

_____

_____

_____

_____

_____

_____

_____

_____

The 2ⁿᵈ Law – Make It Attractive

8. List the previous three good habits using the temptation bundling + habit stacking method. Use the sentence structure: "After [Current Habit], I will [Habit I Need]. After [Habit I Need], I will [Habit I Want]."

_____

_____

_____

_____

_____

_____

_____

_____

_____

The 2nd Law – Make It Attractive

9. What groups could you join in order to help you build your good habits?

_____

_____

_____

_____

_____

_____

_____

_____

_____

The 2nd Law – Make It Attractive

10. For the bad habit you listed previously, what is the deeper desire that the habit is trying to solve? What alternative solution can you develop for that desire?

_____

_____

_____

_____

_____

_____

_____

_____

_____

The 3rd Law – Make It Easy

11. How can you redesign your environment so that your good habits require the least effort possible?

_____

_____

_____

_____

_____

_____

_____

_____

_____

The 3rd Law – Make It Easy

12. For the three good habits that you listed previously, what two-minute task can you complete to start building momentum with that habit?

_____

_____

_____

_____

_____

_____

_____

_____

_____

The 3rd Law – Make It Easy

13. For the bad habit listed previously, what commitment
    device can you develop to prevent you from falling into
    the habit?

_____

_____

_____

_____

_____

_____

_____

_____

_____

The 4th Law – Make It Satisfying

14. For the three good habits you listed previously, what reward can you implement to bring immediate satisfaction?

_____

_____

_____

_____

_____

_____

_____

_____

_____

The 4th Law – Make It Satisfying

15. Which habits will you assess using the habit tracking method?

_____

_____

_____

_____

_____

_____

_____

_____

_____

The 4th Law – Make It Satisfying

16. Write a habit contract listing the habits you want to develop and the immediate consequences for not sticking to the habit. Find 1-2 accountability partners to sign the contract.

_____

_____

_____

_____

_____

_____

_____

_____

_____

_____

Advanced Tactics

17. What areas of work and life satisfy you the most? How can you challenge yourself in each area at the edge of your ability?

_____

_____

_____

_____

_____

_____

_____

_____

_____

Advanced Tactics

18. How often will you reflect on your habits? What questions will you ask to ensure that you are living in alignment with your values?

_____

_____

_____

_____

_____

_____

_____

_____

_____

The One Minute Action Guide

The Fundamentals: Habits involve four steps: Cue, craving, response, and reward. In order to form a good habit, you must make the habit obvious, attractive, easy, and satisfying. To change a bad habit, you must make the habit invisible, unattractive, difficult, and unsatisfying.

The 1st Law – Make It Obvious: Create a Habits Scorecard by listing your daily habits and marking each habit with (+), (-), or (=). Make the cues for those habits obvious by using implementation intention or habit stacking. Implementation intention uses the sentence structure: "I will [Behavior] at [Time] in [Location]." Habit stacking uses the sentence structure: "After [Current Habit], I will [New Habit]."

The 2nd Law – Make It Attractive: Utilize temptation bundling to make a habit attractive. Temptation bundling uses the sentence structure: "After [Current Habit], I will [Habit I Need]. After [Habit I Need], I will [Habit I Want]." Join groups of likeminded people who are performing the habit you want to develop.

The 3rd Law – Make It Easy: Ensure that you are taking action rather than just being in motion. Design your home and work environment to eliminate any obstacles to performing good habits. When starting a habit, keep the duration of the task to two minutes or less.

The 4th Law – Make It Satisfying: Reward yourself with incentives that provide immediate satisfaction. Implement habit tracking to give yourself a sense of accomplishment when you complete a task. Create a habit contract and find an accountability partner to keep yourself from falling back into bad habits.

Advanced Tactics: Find activities that you enjoy and challenge yourself at the limits of your current abilities. Periodically review your progress to ensure that you are staying on track.

Made in the USA
Middletown, DE
18 December 2019